Body, Mind, and Solo

Body, Mind, and Solo

Seven Keys to Conquering
the World Alone

Teresa Rodriguez

BALBOA.
PRESS
A DIVISION OF HAY HOUSE

ISBN: 978-1-4525-5070-1 (sc)
ISBN: 978-1-4525-5068-8 (hc)
ISBN: 978-1-4525-5069-5 (e)

Balboa Press books may be ordered through booksellers or by contacting:
Balboa Press
A Division of Hay House
1663 Liberty Drive
Bloomington, IN 47403
www.balboapress.com
1-(877) 407-4847

Printed in the United States of America

Library of Congress Control Number: 2012907228

Balboa Press rev. date: 11/27/2012

For my mom

No matter where I am
I look up and see
the moon
which reminds me
of your love

Contents

Preface

My story

It was stupid to think that at 19 years of age I had any business getting married. But I did, in a courthouse near San Francisco. He was a tall, gorgeous blonde from Australia and his blue eyes sparkled with hope of a beautiful life "Down Under." Marriage was a part of the Dream that I was sold as a young girl. "You are no one without a husband." So, I dutifully took my place in the realm of the wed and moved to Oz. My goal was to return to California for a Big White Wedding. So, a year after being married and moving to Australia, I returned home to plan the Big Event. Much to my surprise, I received a 6-page letter from him just days after my arrival home. This was in 1989–before cell phones, email, and the Internet. The letter was blunt and painful. "Don't bother coming back to Australia. You're not wanted here. I don't love you. I've moved and disconnected the phone." With the turning of each page I fell deeper into the darkness. The sheets of paper cutting deep into my heart and tearing up any shred of hope I had for my future. Yes, I was young, but I was in love, passionate, and I moved across the planet for a man. My world crumbled. All that I owned, including all my money, was in Australia. Stuck, alone, and lost I fell into a deep depression.

For weeks I visited a psychiatrist every other weekday; each visit ending with the gifting of two valiums–one for that night and one for the following night. After a month of care, I did not improve. I was suicidal, lost over 15 pounds, and the doctor feared that I would harm myself. She handed me a stack of papers after one of our sessions and told me that she was recommending that I spend some time in in-patient care. "There is a lovely facility in the rolling hills of Martinez, California." Fill out this paperwork and bring it with you to our appointment next week. I knew that I was heartbroken, but I did not realize how far into the darkness I let this breakup take me. Shocked, I left the hospital with the stack of papers that weighed down my heart and soul. "This can't be happening to me." I whispered to myself. I looked up with my tear-filled eyes, there a flock of blackbirds danced above me in perfect synchronicity. They swooped down, shining like black confetti, and twirled up to the heavens. I took a deep, cleansing breath and remembered the poem from Ken Kesey's *One Flew Over the Cuckoo's Nest*. "One flew east. One flew west. And one flew over the cuckoo's nest." This was it. I had a choice to accept this lunatic's fate, or I could rewrite the ending. Yes, I was heartbroken. Yes, I was abandoned. Yes, I was broken. But I was still able to choose my fate, and I chose courage. That night I went to a student travel agent and found a trip to Europe. I took the money that I saved for my wedding and bought a ticket to Heathrow. It was my first step to healing and it was through travel that I was able to mend my broken heart and bruised soul.

On my trip I learned that I can rely on myself and that I can trust my intuition. I met wonderful people who helped me recover and taught me how to laugh again. Crazy, I had to travel the world to find myself. But I did. So, if you are a bit lost, broken hearted, or needing some inspiration to move to the next place in your life, I hope that this book brings you the courage you need to move forward with joy and hope.

"A journey of a thousand miles begins with a single step."

- Lao-tzu

May this be your first step.

Teresa

Introduction
Your Journey and This Book

"Throw your dreams into space like a kite, and you do not know
what it will bring back,
a new life, a new friend, a new love, a new country."

- Anaïs Nin

Today, the average life span for those of us living in the wonderful, western world is about 25,550 glorious days. Now, of course, there's a ton of things that can affect how long we live, but more importantly it's not how long we live but how much we live. For example, do you go through your day sentenced to the same drab, monochromatic routine, or are you out there painting your world with neon colors and filling your days with outrageous acts? Good news, even if you tend to wilt towards the more drab existence, my hope is this tiny book will prepare you for some great life-empowering solos trip to places you have always dreamed of going. *Body, Mind, and Solo* challenges you to take a few of your precious days and expand beyond your city limits or time zone and go somewhere out of the ordinary by yourself. Scary? Heck yeah! Worthwhile, fulfilling, and thought-provoking? You bet!

I use "travel" as my metaphor for change and empowerment. Maybe you know it's time to change your career or end a dysfunctional relationship. With any life-changing moment, travel can be the one and only action that you can take that starts the wheels of change and renewal going. It does not have to be a yearlong *Eat, Pray, Love* experience. It can be a simple weekend away without your computer, dramas, and expectations.

If you're searching for a travel guide with the best places to stay in Brazil or information about delicious dim sum in Hong Kong, then you better put this book down, honey. Oh yes, this book is dedicated to all you fabulous women who just can't wait to get out and navigate time zones and flirt with foreign currency. But this is the book you read before you read those other travel books. Think of this lovely little morsel as your travel aperitif, something to cleanse your emotional palette before you sink your teeth into conquering the world alone. This book takes you on a wild ride through your thoughts and emotions, way before you physically jump on a plane, train or rocket ship.

Consider *Body, Mind, and Solo* your pre-flight playground, a place where you can do mental cartwheels and emotional summersaults in preparation for your grand solo adventure. While reading this book, you'll be asked to leap into your thoughts and write down your feelings. This is a very important part of the process, just like you can't order a meal without seeing a menu; you can't plan a trip without reviewing your mental menu of needs and desires. Travel is not a passive act; nor is reading this book. Get into the pages, question your thoughts, explore your imagination and write, write, write! If you need more space—great! Lesson number one - don't let the confines of the pages in this book stop you from starting your own great epic tale. My friend, this is your journey, I'm just here to help you get started; you're the true hero in this traveler's tale.

My hope is that you'll use *Body, Mind, and Solo* as the launching pad to successful solo travel. With the help of these seven short chapters, you'll dig through the stigma and clutter that holds you back from trekking the world—or your city with confidence. Funny enough, the two issues that most people have with traveling solo are being alone and entering the unknown. In Eckart Tolle's bestseller,

The Power of Now, he discusses how most people live in the past or the future and not in the present. His reasoning for this tragedy is that we're afraid of the future, so we view it through the eyes of our past, all the while avoiding the present. When living in that space, we don't have to worry about the strange or unfamiliar because we have so carefully labeled everything in our cautious lives.

We all have done this—created behaviors or beliefs based on our past. Take, for example, my favorite, "All men are assholes." Really, is that true? Or do we base our beliefs on the bad things that have happened to us in the past? Oh yes, I've had a few Casanovas break my heart, and I've spent time licking my wounds covered in Chunky Monkey ice cream. Fortunately, thanks to all my solo travel and learning to live in the now, I've been able to fall in love over and over again—especially with men sporting sexy accents!

When we travel alone, we are forced into the present by the sheer act of having to rely on ourselves and being ever-present with all the distractions and diversities that a foreign place has to offer. That's living in the now, and that's what this book will help you to do by using solo travel as your tool. Mr. Tolle explains that it's only when we exist in the present do we truly begin to live and manifest the life we dream of. Now I can't promise that you'll get everything you want after your first solo voyage, but I can promise you that you'll learn a ton about yourself on the journey and will gain a stronger, more powerful understanding of the crazy, fabulous, nonsensical planet we all live on.

Jackie from San Francisco poetically shares her moment of *now* she found in a small town on the Pacific Ocean: "Carmel By-The-Sea is lovely for a meditation retreat. Through deep breath and inner expansion, I remember the beauty of being soft and open. Life becomes a strange and colorful dance. There is no future, there is no past. There's just the present moment, something for which to be truly grateful."

THE GOAL

By the time you finish this book, you'll learn to overcome the fears that stop you from seeking new experiences in new places alone. Also, you'll have a clear sense of where you want to go and why, and you'll have all the right attitudes it takes to have a great solo adventure. Traveling alone takes more courage, strength, time, and thoughtfulness than traveling with others. But, hey, if you wanted to follow the crowds you wouldn't be reading this book!

I wrote this book to assist you in navigating through the perils of solo travel. Read this book knowing that you'll gain more than just a new stamp in your passport, you'll acquire a fresh perspective of society and an enhanced understanding of the world. And hopefully, with all this jet setting and country hopping, you'll have a newfound appreciation for other cultures and diverse ways of life.

HOW IT WORKS

This book has seven short chapters and you should plan on reading them before you embark on your great adventure. Each chapter explores a specific aspect of solo travel: What do you want? How can you find it? What you need to leave behind, what attitudes are necessary to have a fabulous trip...etc. Within each of these chapters, you'll find room for personal journaling. This is where your own fabulous story begins! My aim is that you'll really think about the questions in each chapter and begin to write your epic tale! Why live vicariously through others? It's your turn to explore, discover, and go beyond the boundaries of solo travel stigma. This moment is yours and this book has been created to take you higher and farther than you've been.

Yes, you can travel alone without this book. As a matter of fact, there are plenty of books that focus on what to pack and where to go. But these pages are not filled with advice on where you should go, but HOW you should go. Through each chapter, you'll gain confidence to let go of the fear of traveling alone and reach for the hope of discovering your divine voice, personal freedom, and creative imagination. Big expectations? Yep.

"Only those who will risk going too far
can possibly find out how far one can go."
- T.S. Eliot

NOW WHAT?

Grab a warm cup of tea, or glass of champagne and a trusty writing companion. I prefer pencils, but whatever you want to use to fill these pages with your own dreams is great. Crayons, pens, plumes, or chalk will work–it's your saga after all! Take at least a day for each chapter. Don't rush ahead. Think about what each sections represents and how it resonates with you. Bring this book along when going through your daily routines; if a spark of inspiration hits, you'll have the book to write your thought down in. Nothing is worse than a lost brilliant thought, expect lost luggage. There are no other rules here, this is you time to explore your world and connect to the most important person on the planet. You!

Have fun!

CHAPTER 1

Be Brave

"I hope that the trip will be the best journey of all journeys;
a journey into ourselves."
- Shirley MacLaine

"I was so afraid the first time I traveled alone. While on my way to
Vancouver, all my fears surfaced. I thought, 'What if I get lonely, or bored,
or what will happen when I eat alone—people will think I'm a loser, who
will I talk with, why am I doing this to myself? I must be crazy!' It took
only one day in the warm sunlight of Vancouver for me to realize that I
was over-reacting. I came to realize that I am a part of a bigger picture,
a global plan, and that—as much as I didn't want to admit it—I'm not the
center of the universe. No longer is traveling alone about loneliness; now,
it's about freedom. Flying solo is a chance for me to take time for my body,
mind, and spirit and to connect with something larger, more spectacular
than my self."

- Wendy, Baltimore

Teresa Rodriguez

The most frequently asked question I get is, "Why would you ever want to waste your vacation being lonely somewhere?" Unfortunately, we live in a society that values independence, but fears loneliness and alienation. We need to understand that time alone, or solitude, does not equal loneliness or desperation. It can equal a renewed sense of independence and liberty to do what you want. In her book, *The Call of Solitude*, Esther Buccholz writes that in these frenetic times, we need our personal space more than ever. Being alone gives us the power to regulate and observe our lives. It can teach us fortitude and the ability to satisfy our own needs. She also asserts that solitude is a restorer of energy. During solo travel we can get reenergized. For you, that can mean long mornings in bed resting or crazy days meeting new people. However you regain your strength, one thing remains true: this time alone brings forth hope with freedom and individuality. Buccholz describes time alone as fuel for life. We need time to restore our mind, body, and spirit. Through this process, we become better-rounded people. And when that happens, we tend to attract others who want to bask in our glow.

You know, sometimes we don't have the option of traveling with another person, and traveling alone doesn't have to be lonely. In fact, it can be a wonderful, freeing experience, and a journey towards self-discovery. This was the case when I went to Brazil for Carnival, I wanted to be around others who also were high-energy and fun. I invited a few friends to join me for my thirtieth birthday celebration. No one could join me, so instead of canceling this important trip, I went alone. As a solo traveler, I was free to enjoy Rio de Janeiro the way I wanted. I didn't have a flock of friends telling me about their needs, this trip was all about me. Every night, I dressed up in bright Carnival colors and went samba dancing. I loved meeting international travelers who also enjoyed the passionate beats of Brazilian music and dancing in the humid heat of Rio nights. I slept in and spent the days

2

hanging out with my recent acquisitions of global jet setters on the beach, while eating barbecue and drinking Caipiriñas. During my eight-day stay in Brazil, loneliness was the farthest thing from my mind. I had too many fabulous things to do, people to meet, and memories to make. I was energized and filled with life.

One of the greatest assets of solo travel is that all the daily expectations of others are absent during your adventure, and you are free to roam the world without this pressure. Radio talk show host, syndicated columnist and guidebook author Pauline Frommer shares what she treasures about solo travel, "When you travel with another person, you spend a lot of your time focused on that person. It's only polite to do so. The blessing of traveling alone is that it allows you to focus outwards, which allows you (often) to have a richer experience of the destination."

It is during your solo voyage that you will have time to think about what *you* need. Does your mind need to stop thinking about work? Does your spirit need some time to recharge? Do you need to rest or rejuvenate your body?

In this chapter we are going to talk about the mind-body-spirit connection and how solo travel can nurture these three areas of your life. I have defined them in the following terms:

- *Mind* is the thinking, feeling part of you; this is where you make conscious decisions and keep mental track of your life. This part can stop working when we try to fill it till it breaks.

- *Body* is your actual physical space and the pace at which you move with your body; this is the part of you that the world sees. You only have one body, so it's best to keep it in tip-top shape, and solo travel helps you do that.

3

- *Spirit* is your essence. It is that element of you that dreams and has desires; it's the intuitive intelligence that burns within you. It's the part of you that is connected to the universe, God, and all creation.

MIND

"A trip is what you take when you can't take any more of what
you've been taking."
- Adeline Ainsworth

How many times have you felt like your brain is about to explode? A good indicator that you need some time alone is when your headaches take up more of your day than your fantasies and daydreaming. It seems that we spend our days organizing, scheduling, and regulating everything around us. And during all this mind-numbing stuff, it's hard for us to find the time to just relax and let our minds wander where they wish. Sue from Half Moon Bay, California shares that when she wants to stop thinking, she travels alone to retreats and/or destinations where she won't have to think. Sue is a social worker in San Francisco and has made a career of assisting others; her solo trips are her time to help herself. "I try to get away at least once a year and clear my head of all the stuff that clutters my mind," she says. For me, it's a much-needed brain dump. I enjoy going to places where I can practice my sketching–that really frees my mind. I usually try to do this at a meditation resort, or a place I know I can spend time alone. By the time I get home, I am a new person; my mind is clear of all the junk I was carrying around and I feel lighter. My husband loves it too, because when I get home I am so much more calm and relaxed.

This philosophy of mind clearing was noted in Ann Japenga's recent *Health* magazine article "The Pleasure of Solitude." Japenga writes about the importance of spending time alone and doing things for yourself. She says that getting out alone is an important aspect to developing a healthy psyche, allowing time to reflect on one's life without the distractions other people present. Relationships, and the need to interact, are also vital aspects to health, but clearing one's head with time alone should not be overlooked. With solo travel you have an opportunity to switch off your roles and responsibilities, and to focus on yourself. It might be hard at first, especially when you've got a nagging boss, screaming kids, and a hungry husband. But you've got to start somewhere, and this place is as good as any.

What does your mind need to let go of before you embark on this trip?

_____

_____

_____

_____

_____

_____

_____

_____

What roles do you need to leave at home to have a beautiful experience? Mom, wife, co-worker?

_____

_____

_____

_____

_____

_____

_____

Teresa Rodriguez

_____

_____

Do you need to find peace or get empowered?

_____

_____

_____

_____

_____

_____

_____

BODY

"Never be afraid to tread the path alone.
Know which is your path
And follow it wherever
It may lead you;
Do not feel you have to
follow in someone else's
Footsteps."
– Eileen Caddy,
Footprints on the Path

Girl, it's time to move that body! When I talk about your body, I mean bits and pieces that incorporates all things physical during your trip. This includes your actual body, the pace at which you like to do things, as well as the places you want to go. During our daily lives, it's our job, family, friends, and commitments that have the Vulcan body grip on our bodies—not us. Would we all go to work at

9:00 a.m. if we had a choice? I wouldn't. My day would start around 11:00 am and end at 8:00 pm, I'm a night person and my body works better on that schedule. Hallelujah there's solo travel. So any time I just want to be my own body boss, I trek off for a few days and listen to my body talk to me.

Verena lives in Palo Alto, California, with her husband and four children. She's a passionate mother and world travelers. She immigrated to the United States from Germany four years ago. Between raising her four children, running an art program for kids, and writing her own nonfiction pieces, she can't wait to get away on her annual solo adventures. Her favorite places to go are up to the mountains and back to Germany. Verena offers a wonderful explanation for why she enjoys solo travel: "When I travel alone I can go at my own pace. I don't need to walk as slow as a toddler, nor do I have to eat as fast as a ten-year-old. I can walk briskly and eat slowly." For one week a year, she allows herself to go at her pace, not at the pace dictated by her children.

> *"The body is a sacred garment."*
> - Martha Graham

Don't forget that your body runs at a different speed than others, and that this can be really frustrating when traveling with others. Before Nancy left for London with her close friend Joanna, she really didn't think about Joanna's activity level—or lack of it. Nancy is a runner and loves art; she was looking forward to hitting the streets of London and checking out all the museums. But she chose a travel partner with a different pace than hers, and her vacation was not all she was hoping for. "I love Joanna, I do," she says. "But that girl walks slower than a snail in quicksand and all I wanted to do was run around town—there's so much to see in London! I like walking fast, talking fast, and eating dinner very slow. Joanna is the complete opposite. We've been friends since college, and we had a blast in school, but my trip to London with her wasn't what I was hoping for. I wanted to dash around London, taking the tube to museums and window-shopping. Not her. She wanted to sleep in and stroll through town at the pace of a three-legged dog. I felt like I was on slow motion for the week. It was very frustrating." Nancy later admitted that she should have done this trip solo. Today her fears of traveling alone have been replaced by the wonderful prospect of running around a new city at her usual frenetic pace.

It's not only tempo that's important when you travel alone; setting you own daily schedule allows you to do the things you really want. You'll enjoy coming and going as you please, with no one demanding your time or attention. Perhaps you want to go shopping one day, and spend the next at a spa—when you travel alone, you can! You can change your mind, change your plans, change your clothes, and do what you want without worrying about disappointing anyone. If rushing around town is not your idea of a vacation, that's fine. Feel free to relax; this is your time to go at your own pace.

Maureen finds traveling alone a wonderful time for self-indulgence. She is married with two grown daughters and usually spends her vacations with them, doing what they like. "I enjoy traveling with my family," she says, "but sometime I like to get away and just take time to go at my own speed—I love sitting in cafés, watching people. I'll bring a book to read or my journal, and order a big steamy cup of hot chocolate and sit back and savor this time with myself."

Sara shares, "My favorite thing to do when I travel alone is sleep as late as I want. When I'm at home, I get up at the crack of dawn, get the family ready, and scramble to get to work. Even when I go on vacation with my family, I'm expected to get up first and get things organized for the day. I need a vacation from my vacations! But when I travel alone, I relish sleeping until I wake and I always treat myself to breakfast in bed."

These women have learned the art of self-satisfaction through traveling alone. Now, this solo journey is your opportunity to listen to what your body wants and needs.

Sit for a minute and ask your body, "Body what do you need?" Rest? Play? Outdoors?

_____

_____

_____

_____

_____

_____

_____

_____

How are you going to honor your body's needs?

_____

_____

_____

_____

_____

_____

_____

_____

How will your body reward you?

_____

_____

_____

_____

_____

_____

_____

SPIRIT

> *"Be not the slave of your own past-*
> *plunge into the sublime seas,*
> *dive deep, and swim far,*
> *so you shall come back*
> *with self-respect,*
> *with new power,*
> *with an advanced experience,*
> *that shall explain*
> *and overlook*
> *the old."*
> —Ralph Waldo Emerson

When I asked my dear mentor and friend, Father Miles O'Brien Riley, who is a retired priest and a former counselor at Canyon Ranch, what he defines as "Spirit," his eyes grew wide, a beautiful bright smile crossed his face, and he shared his thoughts with me like an ebullient child Christmas morning. "My dear Teresa, the word spirituality comes from the Latin 'spiritus' which means 'breath.' In

Greek, 'pneuma.' In Hebrew, the closest word may be 'ruah' which refers to the creative 'ahhh' or breath of God, the energizing divine wind hovering over the waters at the birth of all life. Other words for spirituality include awareness, aliveness, wholeness, holiness, centeredness, openness to the transcendent, and mysticism. And, as much as our mind and body need to be nurtured, so does our spirit. Spirit is the chi, the grace-filled energy, the creative ah-ha that frees us to take the ultimate solo journey -- not around the globe -- but to the depths of our souls."

We need to cultivate the energy and spirit within us, and one way to honor our spirit is through solitude. By nurturing a oneness of the mind, the body, and the spirit, we have the chance to learn more deeply about who we are. Solo travel allows you the freedom to dive into your soul and search for your own personal meaning.

Anne, a close friend and management consultant for Fortune 500 companies, calls these moments alone "miracle moments." She says, "When I travel alone, I allow myself to open up in a way I would never do when I am at home, or with my clients. I let my spirit expand and let that expansion take me over. It's in moments like these that I feel like I've experienced a miracle. Things work out better than I expect, events become more serendipitous, and strangers turn into friends. My spirit longs for these moments and I honor that need with time alone." Anne makes an important point about how our perceptions and expectations naturally change when we fly solo; we only need to deal with our own observation about our environment and ourselves. Who cares what your boyfriend thinks, he's not on this trip with you. For once you can let your spirit soar.

"Life shrinks or expands in proportion to one's courage."
- Anais Nin

11

While living our daily lives, we get caught up in others' perception of us. We are the Friend, the Mother, the Employee, the Sister, and the Wife. We need to step away from these roles and allow our spirit the freedom to ignite. When we get in touch with our inner fire, we are able to find that person we long to be. This is very powerful, and I recommend that while traveling, you be the spirited version of yourself you have hidden deep within you. Have fun with it, be that movie star you've always long to be. Don't be surprised if you come back as that new and improved version of yourself.

Rosa, a sassy single in Sacramento, found this to be true. She observes: "I work for the state of California and my job is pretty stuffy. Even though I see myself as a spicy Latina, while at work, I behave, dress, and talk as Anglo as the next person. But when I travel, I pack my brightest clothes, and the biggest Latina smile you'll ever see. When I'm on vacation, I'm the person I want to be, the Rosa who loves laughing loud, dancing, and eating with sheer pleasure. I hope one day I'll be able to live my spirited self, but until then, I'll keep flying solo." Like Rosa, when you go alone, it is all about you, fulfilling your desires and nurturing your spirit.

Sit with your eyes closed, take a deep breath and let your soul speak. If your spirit was a little girl, what does she need from you?

What will make your spirit soar? More laughter? Dancing? Meditating?

_____

_____

_____

_____

_____

_____

_____

_____

What steps will you take on this journey to honor your spirit?

_____

_____

_____

_____

_____

_____

_____

"Every now and then go away, have a little relaxation,
for when you come back to your work
your judgment will be surer; since to remain constantly at work will
cause you to lose power of judgment."

– Leonardo da Vinci

Give yourself an opportunity to step back from your daily responsibilities. Allow yourself the chance to fly away for a day, a few days, a week, or three weeks—whatever it takes for your body, mind, and spirit to rejuvenate. No projection, no analyzing, no dissecting. Just enjoying. Traveling alone is like eating a mango in the bathtub—you can enjoy soaking in warm water while mango juice runs down your face into the bath. And you don't need to worry; nobody's watching.

"I think that where your journey takes you, there are new gods
waiting there,
with divine patience–and laughter."
- Susan M. Watkins

CHAPTER 2

Be Faithful

"I feel there is something unexplored about a
woman that only a woman can explore."
- Georgia O'Keeffe

"I've never thought about what I want. When I sit and think about
what I want, I get uncomfortable—that same uncomfortable feeling I get
when I dream about going to church in a slip. I don't think anyone has ever
asked me what I want. Good question. What do I want?"

- Helen, Athens

Take a seat Helen; it's your time to have some fun. To truly have a rewarding life, we need to honestly ask ourselves what we want. And because this trip is all about your needs, you have a chance to be self-centered! With travel, there are two things that get overlooked quite often. The first is what your *expectations* are for this trip—what do you really want to get out this adventure? Failing to define your expectations is akin to going to dinner and letting your waiter order his favorite meal for you, then disliking your dinner and blaming him for his poor choice in epicurean delights. Had you given your waiter clues—that you wanted to eat something light, that you love fresh vegetables and fish, but don't like pasta or tomatoes—you would have been far more likely to enjoy your meal. The second overlooked element is what destinations are able to *fulfill* your expectations. Once you have a clearer idea about what type of trip will satisfy your needs, you can focus on finding a location that is well-suited to you. The situation is a lot like dating: you already know what kind of men you like, and if you like tall blond men with fabulous physiques, it is unlikely that Mr. Right will be short, dark-haired, and beer-bellied. Destinations are much the same. You want to be there, or you don't. So, it's time for you to be faithful to your needs and desires and follow your heart.

The first mistake many new solo travelers make is relying on the recommendations of others. This was the case when Bethany from Portland asked friends for advice on destinations for her first solo voyage. Bethany is twenty-eight, works in marketing, and is happily single. When she asked a few friends who were already married with kids where they enjoyed going, many of them said Maui. She excitedly booked her trip to Maui, with a hotel in the coastal city of Waialua, where her friends had stayed. When she got there she was shocked. She had expected to meet fun singles, hang out on the beach, and go on adventure tours. What she found was the complete antithesis of her *expectations*; the coastal town was brimming with newlyweds and families. Everywhere she went, she was met with a room full of happily married couples or families with obnoxious kids. Bethany is an outgoing, friendly person, but she found it very difficult to meet others. She didn't find many who wanted to hang out with an attractive single. (Well, a few guys did, but their wives didn't think too much of that idea.)

Although this trip was not Bethany's ideal vacation, she did learn from her experience. Now, she defines her expectations before traveling. Of course, being alone in a beautiful setting might be your ideal vacation; you might not care if the place is littered with couples because you plan on spending time alone with a few good books. Whatever the case, the goal of this chapter is to help you decide what you truly want from your vacation through answering a series of simple questions. Once you complete this chapter, you'll have a clearer idea about what will make you happy on this trip. And that is what flying solo is all about—your happiness.

First, you'll learn how your personality influences your destination and travel style. Then we'll discuss how to research the most appropriate locations based on your expectations. You'll also learn how to review the reviewer when researching locations via books, online resources, magazine articles, and newspapers. Once you've completed this chapter, you'll have designed the kind of experience you really crave along with a few suitable destinations that will satisfy your desires.

> "Go confidently
> In the direction of your dreams!
> Live the life you've imagined."
> – Henry David Thoreau

Amanda from Los Angeles shares her journey: "I've spent my life organizing family vacations. Once the kids left for college and my husband and I divorced, I found myself alone, but still wanting to explore. All the trips I planned in the past were focused on the desires of the rest of my family. I was just the travel agent, planner, and luggage schlepper. When I had the chance to travel, I had no idea what I wanted! I had to sit down and think about my *self* – someone

I forgot about for the past 30 years. At first the conversations I had with myself were painful and laced with self-guilt, but I was able to find out what I needed. I needed to go somewhere warm where I could rest and enjoy lounging by the pool while meeting new faces."

In my first book, *FLY SOLO, The 50 Best Places on Earth For a Girl to Travel Alone*, I write about the four key components that can make or break your trip:

- **Cultural Interests:** how much culture and art do you want to experience?
- **Activity Level:** how active do you want to be on this vacation?
- **Weather Expectations:** how important is the weather for you?
- **Social Interaction:** how social do you want to be?

We'll dive into these separately, and you'll have an opportunity to think about yourself and what's important to you on this trip. Remember that all vacations differ, so what is true for this trip will not necessarily be true for your next one. As you move through the four components, rate each based on a one-to-five scale, one being LOW on your list and five being HIGH. I call this four-component score the CAWS rating. Once you know what you want, you can review destinations more easily.

CULTURAL INTERESTS

Lori lives in Santa Fe and loves world history. "Some people think that I am a bit weird because I don't care to take normal vacations to places like the Bahamas or Hawaii." she shares. "I just love ancient civilizations, so when I plan my trips, I plan them around some great place I haven't been. So far I have seen Stonehenge in England, the Mayan ruins in Mexico, and The Acropolis in Athens. My next trip is Machu Picchu. Don't get me wrong, I like sleeping in fine hotels and ordering room service, but I also enjoy learning about the past; I think history rocks!" Lori is someone who would give culture a high rating. Other popular cultural activities include going to museums, fine arts performances like theater and opera, enjoying wine-tasting or epicurean tours, taking educational trips, and visiting archeological sites. Individuals who don't really care about culture tend to take pleasure in other aspects of travel such as sports, weather, and social life. Whatever is true for you, honor that on your next trip.

Rate your Cultural interest level by choosing the **one** statement below that best describes your attitude toward culture on this journey. There is no right or wrong answer:

- The last thing I want to do is see a museum, unless I can bungee jump off the roof.
- If there's time, I might try to find an art gallery, but that's only if my new friends can't join me for lunch.
- I'm headed to the big city, but it's to practice the fine art of shopping!
- Yes, I'll catch a play or two while I'm here, but I also want to check out that new spa I've been hearing so much about.
- Tell me everything! I can't wait to learn all about the politics and history of the area. I'm thinking ten hours of ruins followed by a night at the theatre.

After reading this section, how important is culture to you on this next trip of yours? Be honest! It's all about your needs.

_____
_____
_____

Teresa Rodriguez

Based on your needs what are some activities that will make you happy?

ACTIVITY LEVEL

Many times we don't consider our activity level an important factor in planning a trip. I didn't think about it until I was stuck on a small, but beautiful island in the Great Barrier Reef off Australia. It was a place where couples went away to honeymoon, and hiking, biking, and water sports were not on its list of activities. Sharp coral surrounded the island, and the only way to get to the island was by boat. Where was the wide, sandy beach with lovely, tanned gentlemen giving windsurfing lessons? Although the hotel had a workout room (two stationary bikes and a set of dumbbells), there was little opportunity for outdoor exercise. I went crazy there, and it was then that I realized how important activity is to me. Even just a brisk walk outside or an hour of aerobic training—I need to move!

How important is activity to you during this trip? Do you find darting around exhausting, or does sitting on a beach all day sound like torture? Is this trip about getting into shape, or is it about resting after a few months of stressful work? Do you plan on working out every day, or is this trip about reclining with a good book and a cocktail?

Based on your expectations, rate your activity level now by choosing the **one** statement below that best describes your attitude toward activity on this trip. Remember there is no right or wrong answer here - it's all about your needs:

- I really want to rest on this vacation and I don't plan on moving from my beach chair or cozy recliner for a week.
- I'd enjoy walking along cobblestone streets, too narrow for cars.
- I'd be open to trying a new sport like surfing one day.
- Yes, I want to get my heart rate up, and I would like to hit the gym a few times .
- Definitely! I'm all about extreme sports, I'm ready for a kayaking or cycling trip.

Are you ready to dive into a week of exercise and adventure, or are you leaning towards a vacation filled with rest and relaxation? Describe your perfect trip here:

_____

_____

What are the steps you need to take to make sure that you have what you need for your activity level? Pack romance novels? Pack hiking gear?

_____

_____

_____

_____

_____

_____

_____

"The indispensable first step to getting the things you want out of life is this:
decide what you want."
-Ben Stein

WEATHER EXPECTATIONS

I'm planning a trip right now and my top priority is the weather. A warm breeze, a nice hint of sunshine on my shoulders, and a cool cocktail resting on the sand by my stacks of must-read magazines sound like heaven. It's winter where I live, and I'm getting a bit bored with chapped lips and pale skin, so I'm looking for destinations that can guarantee me temperatures in the high 70s during the day. In the past, this hasn't been the case. I usually look for places that are high in culture, where I can stroll through museums during the day, enjoy lovely meals, and scoot off to the theater at night—without regard to the temperature. But this trip is different, and I'm determined to find a destination where I can recline on a white, sandy beach, get a lovely bronze tan, and wear cute, revealing dresses at night.

Of all the things that can affect your vacation, climate is the one that can dampen your trip the most - if you are not prepared. When Judy from Baltimore planned her trip to the Bahamas, her goal was to get out of the harsh Maryland winter. Unfortunately, she didn't check the weather before she booked her trip. It's usually very lovely there, except during hurricane season.

When deciding how important the weather is to your trip, consider what time of year you plan to travel. Don't expect the sun to be out just because you're going on vacation. Check out weather. com for comprehensive weather reports, put in your destination of choice and when you want to go. There you can find the average temperatures for the month you plan to visit. I found this very helpful when choosing a warm destination for my Christmas holiday. For the three final destinations I chose, I looked up the past's year's average temperature for the same weeks I was going to be there. Cancun and the Mayan Riviera won, with an average daily temperature of 81 degrees. It tends to rain for an hour or so every few days, in the afternoon, so I'll make sure to pack a light jacket. Research and thoughtful planning can ensure that you have the kind of vacation you're craving and that you've packed the appropriate clothes.

Now, rate your weather expectations by choosing the **one** statement that best describes your attitude toward weather and climate for this trip:

+ I want to go somewhere rich in history (or whatever component is most important to you) and I don't care about the weather.

- Nice weather can be a plus, but if I find out the weather is less than perfect during my planned trip, I won't change my itinerary.
- Yes, weather is a big factor for me. I want to be somewhere (warm, cold, hot, etc) and I will choose a location that will fit my expectations.
- Definitely! I need (warm, cold, hot, etc.) and I am choosing my destination based on the weather. If the weather is not what I expect, I will be very disappointed.
- The only reason I am on this trip is because of the climate and weather conditions.

Answering 1 means that weather in NOT a factor for you on this trip. Answering 5 means weather is a VERY IMPORTANT factor and if the weather is not what you want, then it could ruin your experience.

Will the weather affect your enjoyment of this trip? Write down your thoughts.

_____

_____

_____

_____

_____

_____

_____

_____

What will you do if the weather is not the way you wanted? How can you manage your expectations and still have a wonderful time?

_____

_____

_____

_____

_____

_____

_____

_____

"He never is alone that is accompanied with noble thoughts."
– Fletcher

SOCIAL LEVEL

When you travel alone, you decide how many people you want to meet—or not meet. Very often, we want to get away and spend time with our own thoughts. But other times we want to dress like a movie star and meet new friends while being our spirited selves. Janet, who lives in Kansas City, is considered by her friends to be a shy and conservative intellectual. However, her trip to Greece in 2003 revealed a different side. "After I finished my graduate degree, I decided to take some time off before starting my new career as a researcher for a consulting firm. I sat down in my airplane seat and something changed in me: instead of being scared or self-conscious, I became this outgoing, fun girl from the Midwest. By the time I got off the plane in Athens, I'd met three boisterous girls from a small town outside of Kansas City who were staying in the hotel down the street, and we planned to meet for dinner that evening. I bought little sun dresses and danced the nights away. I even met a guy from Italy who spent a semester at the University of Kansas and didn't understand why KU's football mascot looks like a chicken. We spent a day taking a bus tour to the Parthenon and sharing stories of the Midwest. Now, when I take my vacations, I tend to go places where I know I can meet a ton of people and where there's a social nightlife."

Although Janet enjoys high social interaction on her trips, many women are looking for a bit of peace and alone time on their vacation. Diane from Houston is one of these women. "I am a high school teacher with twin daughters who are about to enter middle school," she explains. "When I get a chance to retreat from the world for a few days, I want to be left alone. I let others know where I am, but I just want some time to regroup and spend moments thinking in silence. During the year, I collect books and magazines I want to read when I go away. I have this little pile in the corner of my office and I smile every time I see it, because it's my reminder that I'll be getting away one day to read it all—and I do!"

Do you want to meet new people, or do you want to spend time alone? Are you interested in taking tours, or do you want to do things completely on your own? Or would a combination of both make you happy? Can you see yourself spending time alone in a museum, but looking forward to a group tour a bit later on? Take time to play each scenario out in your mind.

Rate your social expectations by choosing the **one** statement below that best describes your attitude about social activity for this journey:

+ No, I don't want to meet a soul. This trip is about spending time alone with a few good books and my thoughts.
+ I would prefer time alone, but if I end up meeting a few fun souls then I'll be up for some fun.

- If I meet people fine, if not, no big deal. And I won't write off a location if it's buzzing with people either.
- Yes, I would like to meet new people. I want to go someplace where I can spend some time with new friends.
- Yes! I need people around me all the time. I want to make new friends and do things with others.

Choosing 1 means you want to be totally alone and so you won't worry about choosing a location because of others there. Choosing 5 means that you would wither if left alone, make sure to choose a place with lots of people you can meet.

If you want to be with others, what are some types of people you want to meet?

_____

_____

_____

_____

_____

_____

_____

_____

How will you meet them?

_____

_____

_____

_____

What will happen if you find yourself alone when you want to be with others? How will you loneliness at bay?

If you want to be alone, write about your perfect day.

"Desire creates the power."
– Raymond Holliwell

PUTTING IT ALL TOGETHER

Take a look at your ratings of Cultural Interests, Activity Level, Weather Expectations, and Social Level. By now, you've envisioned yourself walking barefoot, wrapped in a floral sarong on a warm beach, or strolling through the streets of Europe with a latte in one hand and a museum guide in the other. Or are you looking forward to hiking through the rain forest?

With this in mind, brainstorm your answers to the following questions:

Where do you want to go? (Beach, city, village, island, small town)

_____

_____

_____

_____

_____

_____

_____

_____

What are you going to do there? (Rest, read, relax, walk, hike, run, work out, stroll, sail, eat, learn)

_____

_____

Teresa Rodriguez

_____

_____

_____

_____

_____

_____

How social do you want to be? (Meet lots of people, meditate alone, meet a few like-minded friends)

_____

_____

_____

_____

_____

_____

_____

What kind of weather do you want? (I don't care, wonderfully warm, nice and chilly, windy, calm, hot)

_____

_____

_____

_____

_____

_____

_____

This part of your trip planning becomes a process of elimination as well as an exploration of your desires. Perhaps you know that you don't want to go to a big city, and you know you want to be somewhere warm, so you focus on small towns in warm areas. You know you want to work out, so you plan to find a place with a gym, or close to outdoor activities. Finally, you would like to meet new people, so you want to go somewhere social. Quickly looking at these sets of desires, you know you won't be going to Dublin or Toronto in winter!

When I asked my friend Carolyn these questions before she took her annual Christmas vacation, this is what she said: "Perhaps a city for a few days, then off to the beach -- I want to walk around a city and then learn how to scuba dive. I'm not too interested in seeing anything cultural; I did the museums thing last year when I went to Venice (Culture rating: 1). In the city I would like to meet a few people, but no big deal (Social rating: 3); when I'm at the beach, I would like to take scuba lessons (Activity rating: 4), so I'll get to meet a few people there; and I want the weather it to be warm, warm, warm (Weather expectations: 5)" Where would you advise Carolyn to go? I told her to go to Australia. And this is why: she wanted warm weather, which is hard to guarantee in the northern hemisphere during December; she wanted both city (Sydney) and beach (Port Douglas); she wanted to learn to scuba dive, and what better place to do that than the Great Barrier Reef? She had the time and the money, and she had a fabulous vacation in the Land Down Under!

Feel free to check out www.tangodiva.com, where you will find city ratings based on the four components we discussed in this chapter. Also, this is the time you can call on travel agents, friends, and family. Instead of asking them, "Where do you like going on vacation?" say, "I'm interested in taking a trip alone where I can meet interesting, new people (Social), check out museums (Cultural), stay in a hotel where I can work out in the morning (Activity), and I don't care what the weather will be like (Weather)." The responses you get will be much more specific to your needs, because you have made your requests very clear. Travel agents love to talk to clients who have a good sense of what they want to experience. You'll find that once you have a basic list of expectations for your trip, it will be much easier to determine which locations can fulfill your desires.

REVIEWING THE REVIEWS

The easiest way to find the perfect locations is to read what others are saying about various destinations around the world. But, be forewarned: you need to review the reviews to ensure quality control. Who actually wrote the review and would you like this person if you met him/her? Do you have anything in common with this person? Dorothy from Chicago writes: "I learned this lesson after my second bite of a horribly fattening cookie in Hana, Maui. It occurred to me that I needed to take more time reviewing the reviews before going on a trip. I remember reading an in-depth review written by a woman who raved about all the wonderful things to experience in Hana. She wrote about the hair-raising yet beautifully lush drive to the town, the quiet nights, and the fabulous cookies one can buy at the corner store. I should have suspected the reviewer when she wrote a whole paragraph on her beloved to-die-for macadamia nut cookies. When I got home and reread the review, I began to develop an image of the person who wrote the article. Not once did she mention any activities that I enjoy, such as snorkeling or horseback riding. She did mention a small, secluded beach that was hiking distance from the hotel, but the path was too treacherous for her to hike. She said nothing about the hotel service, or the lack thereof. When I look back on her review, I can see that it was written by someone I wouldn't take advice from in my real life. Based on her review, I'd decided to wear my hiking boots, and I looked more like a ridiculous, over-reactive tourist than a savvy, world-class traveler. The trail was a wide, forgiving path that was as flat as a table and smooth with thick black sand. As an active person, this was not a 'hike'; it was a short walk to a secluded beach. I should have done more research into the activities I enjoy before choosing Hana as a destination." Dorothy has no plans to return to Hana.

Because reviews can sometimes be a bit one-sided, or not focused on your personal interests or desires, you should review your destinations using a large selection of sources. It would be great if we all had a personal vacation shopper who knew exactly what we wanted. Thanks to the Internet, you can research destiatnoins and reviews until you are blue in the face. Take time to review the reviews. Find out who wrote them and if you can really trust their reviews. Remember, there is a big difference between travel writing in Town and Country and in Maxim magazine. Books are a great place to get pragmatic facts and statistics on a destination and country. My favorite city and country guides are published by Knopf and Dorling Kindersley. I love their high-style appeal and in-depth historical backgrounds. In these guides, you will find passionate details about the historical relevance of the country and its sites. Plus they look great on coffee tables and book shelves. Other guides I rely on are *Time Out*, for their social and cultural section; *Michelin Guides*, for their basic information; *Frommer's*, for their detailed listings of hotels and restaurants; and *Lonely Planet*, for their sense of adventure. I recommend that you go to a large bookstore, see what they have to offer and see what resonates with you and your style. Also, visit your local library to find books on different destinations, and see what the history and general-interest books have to say about your chosen places.

Online, www.amazon.com has a great selection of travel books, destination topics, and subject guides, so you can search a very large selection quite easily. Make sure to get a few magazines as well. The magazines I rely on are Condé Nast's *Traveler*, *Travel and Leisure*, *Budget Travel*, American Express Platinum's *Departures* magazine, and the travel sections in my favorite fashion and lifestyle magazines.

For website reviews, I first try Google by typing in key terms like the destination, type of hotel I want, and the time of year I want to go. I'm given a random selection of hits that all have one thing in common: my search request. This can be overwhelming, so schedule some time to search online for nuggets of useful information. To weed out places you want to avoid, try inputting negative terms like "bad experience" or "don't go there," and see if anything comes up. Check out newspapers such as the *New York Times*' Sunday travel section, or any metropolitan newspaper's Sunday edition. Visit a travel agent to discuss your *expectations* for your trip, and see what locations he or she recommends. If any locations sound like winners, ask for a brochure or two on each location. By this time, you'll be forming an idea about the locations that will be right for you.

Start researching locations based on your desires. What destinations seem to resonate with you?

_____

_____

_____

_____

_____

_____

_____

What places do you want to avoid?

_____

_____

_____

_____

_____

_____

_____

_____

Where did you research and what did you find that interests you?
Sound bites?

_____

_____

_____

_____

_____

_____

_____

Keep a record of the reviews you find. Which ones inspire you and
which disappoint you?

_____

_____

_____

_____

_____

_____

_____

CHAPTER 3

Be Wise

*"Success is a journey not a destination,
half the fun is getting there."*
– Gita Bellin

*"In 2009, I gave up my life in the US to live in Thailand, a land I had
never been to before, and stayed for 2.5 years. I learned to stay present in
faith, guided by my intuition. When my plans were not what I need for my
growth, I would see the signs that showed me the way. I brought home the
power to create work that I love and the wisdom to stay true to myself."*
- Elicia, San Francisco

Anything that is worth doing takes lots of hard work. There can
be months of planning and savings before you get to go on your
great adventure. Don't worry, your first trip does not have to be a
intense tour to some remote destination. You don't have to start out
on a two month Himalaya trek by yourself; you can work up to it.
World warriors are not made in one trip, but in a lifetime of smart

travel. But, then again, you can create an adventure like Elicia that takes you away for years. Be open to many options.

Imagine yourself touring the countryside with an international group of like-minded people. Perhaps you're all bird watchers or avid cyclists. Picture yourself in a cozy village lodge laughing over meals with new faces, or comparing stories in a riverside resort. Everything has been created for your comfort, and the biggest decision you'll have to make in the morning is coffee or tea. Does this sound enticing? If so, you might be up for a semi-solo vacation. This is how I began my solo travels. I started traveling with a friend, then tried group tours, and worked up to traveling alone to resorts. Each step brought me closer to independent solo traveling.

The world is bursting with all sorts of group trips and destinations for solo travelers. There are plenty of resources that focus on specific trips that might interest you.

Before you choose a group package, tour, or all-inclusive vacation that suits you, you need to ask yourself some important questions:

+ If you are single, are you looking for other singles?

_____

_____

_____

_____

_____

_____

_____

_____

+ Are you in a relationship and just want to get away for
  a few days?

_____

_____

_____

_____

_____

_____

_____

_____

+ Do you want to travel with all women, or is co-ed okay?

_____

_____

_____

_____

_____

_____

_____

+ What kinds of people do you want to meet?

_____

_____

_____

_____

_____

_____

_____

- Do you want this trip to center around physical activities such as biking, hiking, horse riding, or surfing?

_____
_____
_____
_____
_____
_____
_____

- Do you want to learn something on this trip, like cooking or another language?

_____
_____
_____
_____
_____
_____
_____

- Do you want your own room, or are you happy sharing with another person?

_____
_____
_____
_____
_____
_____

These are important questions you need to answer—keep in mind your CAWS preferences. Usually, women who rate Social higher than the other three factors tend to migrate towards tours. If Social is low on your needs, remember that going semi-solo, especially in a group tour, will limit your options. If you want your own space to go where you please, a destination resort might suit your needs better. Tours are great when you're comfortable spending time with the same people for seven to fourteen days.

"I hear and I forget. I see and I remember. I do and I understand."
– Confucius

TOURS

Joan's husband dislikes traveling. He covets his prized English rose garden and spends his free time watching cricket in silence. She had long since mastered the art of English cooking: roast pork, baked potatoes, and fish and chips. But she longed to spend a week in Italy learning how to prepare Italian cuisine. She researched tours that specialized in cooking classes and found one that fit her schedule and price range. "I've never been on a tour like this, and at first I was very nervous" she said. "But my excitement outweighed my fears.

My husband drove me to Heathrow Airport; we didn't talk much on the way. It was a sad drive and I realized that this trip meant more to me than just learning how to cook. This trip represented my ability to venture out; it was about letting go of fear and doing something I always dreamt about. I've been married for twenty-four years and my life's focus was on my husband and our three children. When our son passed away four years ago, we both died with him. My husband retreated to the garden and I withered away in the house. The last time we drove to London was to clean out our son's flat. I thought a lot about my son on the way to the airport, and I believed he would be very proud of me. He always said I should get out more. So, I did. I could just picture him in heaven smiling down on me!

When I arrived in Rome, the tour company had a delightful sign with my name on it–I felt like a movie star. From that moment on, I didn't have to worry about anything. I spent a week in Florence–a culinary paradise–chopping fresh basil, kneading fluffy dough, and tasting robust wines from around Tuscany. Now I understand why the great thinkers of the Renaissances portrayed Florence as heaven–it is! I made new friends, learned cooking secrets, and created delicious food. This tour restored a part of me that had shriveled away. Once again I was a young girl, full of creativity and wonder, learning, growing, and discovering abilities I'd never explored. I wouldn't have been able to do this trip alone, so having a guide and other travelers with me was ideal. I shared my room with a marvelous, kind woman from Canada–she also left her husband at home! I found comfort in my fellow travelers and in the food. Who knew I could make savory braised lamb ravioli with fresh grilled Portabella mushrooms and eggplant! Not only did I learn how to cook like an Italian mama, I met some fabulous women, and healed a part of my broken heart.

When I arrived back in London, my husband was waiting for me. Although I was only gone ten days, I could tell we had both changed. He stood there, like the passionate young man I fell in love with– holding flowers from his garden–and smiling with tears brimming in his eyes. I was aglow, with the smell of lavender and thyme still on my skin. Our hug at the airport was electric. On the way home we talked nonstop. We giggled and chatted about his time alone, how he missed me, and almost starved! And I swooned with stories about my adventures with fresh herbs, olive oil, and pomegranates. We fell in love again. I'm thinking about taking a cooking course in France next year!"

> *"Earth's crammed with heaven."*
> – Elizabeth Barrett Browing

Joan, like many other women, find tours a safe, social, and educational way to travel. Tours are renowned for taking care of all your travel details once you arrives—your transportation, accommodations, meals, sightseeing, etc. Confirm the tour's benefits first, because all tours differ. Make a point to check out local walking tours or historical tours in your city or neighborhood to get a sense of what it's like being with a group. The unfortunate element about tours, especially overseas, is that if you're uncomfortable with the other guests, there is little you can do about it. You can't be assured that some obnoxious, needy traveler is not on your trip. But then again, it is a great opportunity to work on your patience and people skills!

You might want to call the tour company you're thinking about using and find out what types of people usually attend. Ask honest questions about your concerns, and with any luck you'll get candid answers about the tour participants. Also ask about the accommodation setup. Most times you are required to share with another same-sex person. If you want your own room, you'll need to request it, and plan on spending additional cash for this luxury.

This is a good time to do some self-reflection. How are you feeling about tours, do they make you feel safe or stifled?

_____

_____

_____

_____

_____

_____

_____

_____

What are some of your own personal needs that might not get met in a group tour situation?

_____

_____

_____

_____

_____

_____

_____

_____

Can you compromise or do you need to seek another type of travel experience?

_____

_____

_____

_____

_____

_____

_____

_____

"Happiness is not a destination. It is a method of life."
– Burton Hills

DESTINATIONS

Perhaps you're not ready to go solo, but you're not interested in tours. A destination location might be ideal. These would include places such as Club Med, spas, yoga camps, retreats, all-inclusive resorts, and sports camps. Each of these choices tends to cater to a specific demographic.

My first experience with a semi-solo trip was to Club Med. Years and years ago, they had great specials called Wild Cards. For one thousand dollars you could book a seven-day all-inclusive vacation–flight, room, food and drinks! You just did not know where you were going to go until a week before the trip. I booked my reservation not knowing where I would end up. Lucky me, I arrived at Paradise Island in the Bahamas. My roommate, Carolyn, was a fabulous femme who also worked in advertising. She came alone and planned on having a great time socializing with others. We spent the week sharing advertising tales, flirting with guys, and hanging out with twelve other singles we'd met on the trip. How life has changed, both Carolyn and I are moms now.

One of the advantages of destination vacations is the ability to get away from others and spend time alone. You have the autonomy to enjoy your vacation at your own pace. You can take pleasure in quiet walks, or nestle under a palm with a book, as well as socialize with diverse groups of international travelers. Most resorts are packed with activities to keep your day bursting with things to do, so you won't have the chance to get bored or lonely. If you're not good at meeting people, but want to learn how, this can be a great way to begin because many resorts focus on socializing, getting to know other guests, and creating a sense of community.

How are you feeing about going on a semi-solo trip to a resort? Does this feel better or worse than a tour?

_____

_____

_____

_____

_____

_____

_____

_____

When it comes to spending time with others on your vacation, what personality traits of yours will people find enjoyable? (For example, being friendly, energetic, honest, fun loving.)

_____

_____

_____

_____

_____

_____

_____

_____

What are some of the boundaries will you set before booking your trip? Do you want your own room? Will you need time alone?

_____

_____

_____

_____

_____

_____

_____

_____

"Each friend represents a world in us, a world possibly not born until they arrive,
and it is only by this meeting that a new world is born."
– Anais Nin

FRIEND NETWORK

Another fantastic semi-solo option is visiting friends who have moved overseas or somewhere you want to visit. Don't assume that they'll want you to stay with them. Call first, tell them you'd like to visit, and see what they have to say. If they offer you a place to stay, that's a bonus! And if you do stay, make sure you give them their space, privacy, and time to decompress when they get home. Although you're on vacation–they usually aren't. Don't expect your hosts to keep you entertained during your visit. All the rules of solo travel still apply; you're responsible for planning your personal itinerary. After your stay, wash the bed linens and towels you used, buy your hosts a special thank-you gift, and leave their home and the space you occupied a bit cleaner than when you arrived. You want to be remembered as the fabulous woman that you are, especially if it's a destination you want to come back to!

If your plans take you to a place where none of your friends live, send e-mail to everyone you know and ask if *they* know anyone. Let them know where you're going, when you plan to be there, and what you like to do. Get the introduction and take it from there. Ideally, your friends' friends will take you to cool bars, restaurants, shopping streets, cafés, attraction, or at least recommend some.

When Sally from Cork, Ireland decided to go around the world alone, she e-mailed all her friends with her planned itinerary. She asked for names, emails, and numbers of friends living abroad whom she could meet for a meal or contact for local information. By the time she departed Dublin, she had a phone book filled with names from around the world. I met Sally when I was living in Melbourne, Australia. At the time, she was visiting a generous friend who offered her a place to stay for a few nights. I gave her a list of my friends in San Francisco who would be delighted to entertain her. When she got to there, she called them and they treated her to a day of wine tasting in Napa Valley. The next time I caught up with her, this is what she shared:

"This world tour has proved to me that we live on a small, special planet and at the end of the day, we're all friends. I met Teresa in a pub in Melbourne and before I knew it, I was in Napa Valley with four of her friends sipping wine! I've told all the wonderful people I met that if they come out to Cork, they have a place to stay–it might be small, but I always have a few bottles of Guinness in the frig! Now I am very aware that what happens in Brazil–or anywhere else in the world– affects me. I think that's the greatest lesson I learned from traveling–that we're all connected by deep and meaningful relationships. I wish everyone could go on a trip like this. I believe the world would be a better, safer, happier place if everyone got to experience the power of friendships and connections through solo travel." Because of this passion, I started TangoDiva.com. There, you can connect to other women travelers around the world. You can meet women who live where you want to visit. These Tango Diva members serve as enthusiastic resources for other solo women travelers and it is such a delight to hear about Tango Divas meeting up around the globe.

Unfortunately, sometimes your friends don't turn out to be the loving, welcoming hosts you expected. It's smart to have a realistic exit strategy. If things get hard to handle, be able to change your ticket or get a hotel room- you might have a better time spending the cash. Monica shares her story: "I went to visit a friend in Chicago. I have to admit that she wasn't a very close friend; we met at the gym and we both attended the same weekly Pilates class. One day she said she was taking a job in Chicago and that I could visit her any time. I've never been to Chicago, so, I took her up on it. I left my husband and dog at home and headed to Chicago for four days to visit her. What a nightmare. I'm a low-key person and I soon found out that this woman was strung tighter than a banjo! The fours days with her were high-intensity DRAMA. Everything was an issue; she spent our evenings creating a scene everywhere we went – I felt sorry for our waiters and hostesses. I didn't plan on this kind of trip and by the third day, I was ready to go home. I don't wish that on anyone." Situations like this happen, so be prepared with a plan of action – just in case.

HOUSE SITTING

If you're responsible enough to take good care of someone's property and pets while they're away, you might explore the possibility of house sitting. Be prepared to take extra-good care of their home and animals. (Don't forget to water the plants and if something breaks, make sure to share that information with them). Request a list of contact numbers—including their travel itinerary, as well as the number for the vet and a neighbor or friend who lives near by. Remember to leave the house cleaner than it was when you arrived, fill the refrigerator with some of their favorites, and leave a thank you card and flowers—then, you'll have the opportunity to come back again.

As someone who often has people staying at my house when I travel, I like having my house sitter here the day before I depart so I can show them how things work (the house alarm, entertainment system, washing machine, cat feeding details, etc.) and I like them gone right before I arrive home. I appreciate a note, letting me know how their visit was and if anything happened. I set my expectations very high for those who stay at my home, and I only let people stay that I trust with my life.

Trudy from Vancouver has mastered house sitting and now is known as the person to call, because she takes such great care of pets and always leave the homes she sits in mint condition. "The first time I was asked to house sit was when my college friend was going on his honeymoon and they needed someone to take care of their home and animals in Sonoma, California. I was in graduate school, so I had the time to stay at a quiet place and write my thesis. They had three cats and two dogs. I loved those animals like my own and I made sure the house was spick and span when they got home. I treated the animals like royalty and even bathed them. As a wedding gift, I found a landscaper who planted a garden of colorful flowers in their front yard. When they got home, they found a living bouquet of flowers blooming, a refrigerator full of fresh food, five clean and happy pets and a thank you note. They told all their friends about what I did and people who need a pet/house sitter call me every few months. Unfortunately, I don't have the time I did when I was getting my Masters, so I am unable to take advantage of these opportunities. Honestly, it's way more work than just staying in a hotel room, because you're responsible for someone's home and their much-loved pets. I've had accidents happen where pets broke glass objects and fish died. So, my advice is—if you're not interested in the responsibility, don't pet sit."

Doe any of these low-cost travel ideas appeal to you? If so, which ones?

_____

_____

_____

_____

_____

_____

_____
_____

Do you have any friends around the world that you would like to visit?
When can they host you? How long would you stay? What special
gift would you take them or leave for them?

_____
_____
_____
_____
_____
_____
_____

Do you have friends that might need you to house sit? Do they have
pets? What would your responsibilities be?

_____
_____
_____
_____
_____
_____
_____

DELIGHTFUL DETOURS

If you must travel to a wedding, reunion, or business meeting,
take advantage of the opportunity to explore. My friend Ashley is

attending a wedding in Lanai; she is taking a week off before the nuptials and plans on attending an all-girls surf spa. For the first week she'll be flying semi-solo in Oahu, learning how to surf between her manicures, seaweed wraps, and massages. When she arrives at the wedding, she'll be relaxed, tanned, and ready to greet all her relatives—with her perfect mani-pedi and glowing exfoliated skin!

Business travel is another great way to add on a few extra days of sightseeing and exploration. Many times airline tickets are a bit less expensive when you have a Saturday stay. Plan your meetings at the beginning or end of the week so you can take advantage of this nice business travel perk.

Any upcoming work trips that you can take advantage of?

_____

_____

_____

_____

_____

_____

_____

_____

How about family events, weddings, or reunions?

"He never is alone that is accompanied with noble thoughts."
– Fletcher

What resonates with you?

Tours:

- Educational tours
- Cooking classes
- Wine tours
- Yachting tours
- Writing retreats
- Skiing tours
- Cultural tours
- Activity-based tours (i.e. bike across France)
- Other

Destination resorts:

- Sport camps
- Adventure camps
- Spas
- Health resorts
- Clubs
- Snorkel destinations
- Surf camps
- Other

Friends Network

- Visiting a friend
- Going somewhere where I can meet friends of friends
- House/pet sitting

Delightful Detours

- Upcoming required trips
- Free weekends, holiday weekends (long weekends)

Business Travel

- Finding time to stay
- Making a plan to explore

CHAPTER 4

Be Light

"You are the light of the world, a city on a hill that can't be hidden, let you light shine."

– Jesus

"Was I scared? Heck yeah! It's not like you jump out of a perfectly good plane every day. But I'll tell you something: I've never felt so alive in my life! I think everyone should do something that they fear—it's a great way to build your confidence and prove that you are capable of the impossible."

- Candace, Cape Town

As the outfits pile up on my bed and my suitcase trembles at the impending onslaught, I secretly know that on this trip, I'm going to be someone else. The knowledge that I'm leaving some of myself behind makes me feel free, light, and giddy with anticipation. Sure, I may only narrow my luggage down to four pairs of strappy sandals; but when it comes to who I am, I have pared down considerably more. Before every trip, I'm brimming with excitement about the unknown adventure before me, as well as the opportunity to revel in some "me time." I love being a mother, friend, and mentor, but I relish my moments of just being. No title, no name, just an unknown soul wandering the planet, awed by the vastness of life. I go from human *doing* to a human *being*. I'm not the same person when I stroll the streets of Paris in search of the perfect pink stilettos as I am when I rest under the glowing Caribbean sun, lulled to sleep by gentle waves lapping at my toes. I'm pure potential, diving into the moment. This is what I want to bring home in my suitcases: the freedom to live my life the way I live it when I travel. I want that fearlessness, that patience, that ability to forgive, and to smile. I want to always embrace my environment with joy. On this journey of life, I continue to strive to become more like my traveling self. With each trip, I bring back a bit more peace and understanding and I leave behind a few pieces of heavy baggage.

One morning, during a particularly difficult time in my life, I woke from a vivid dream that I was in a garden and wanted to pick some beautiful flowers, but couldn't put down the heavy, cold stones I was carrying. A guardian angel came to me and said that the only way I could ever hold anything beautiful was to let go of the stones. How's that for a powerful metaphor! For we all carry heavy stones. Sometimes in our hands; other times, in our hearts, or minds. All this baggage does is weigh us down—and when we travel alone, we need to travel light. Of all the baggage I carry (and I have plenty!) the three pieces that affect me the most are *fear*, *laziness*, and *pride*. Fear is the emotion that leaves me helpless: I lose all my confidence and imagine only worst-case scenarios. And even I, a seasoned sojourner, still can be lazy when it comes to planning my trips ahead of time to ensure a fun, safe adventure. When I get lazy, my level of fear increases, because I haven't taken the time to prepare well. Pride is a tough one. Sometimes, when I'm going about my day, I get a bit full of myself: this can be problematic when traveling because I find that

I need all the help that I can get—and no one wants to help a snobby prima donna, I've learned to try to be patient and accept the fact that I'm not always right. (As hard as that may be!)

"Challenges make you discover things about yourself that you never really knew. They're what make the instrument stretch—what makes you go beyond the norm."
– Cicely Tyson

In Louise Hay's *You Can Heal Your Life*, she outlines the symptoms of fear. "Fear," she writes, "is by far the biggest category of resistance—fear of the unknown." It's this fear of the unknown that holds us back from making a voyage. As Marie Curie said, "Nothing in life is to be feared. It is only to be understood." If anyone knew about fear, it was Marie. She was rocking the science world in Russian-occupied Warsaw in the 1800's even as she dealt with sexism, war, and poverty. She attended the fledgling Flying University, a secret academy for young women who wanted to take college-level courses but were unable to travel abroad. The classes were held in private residences around the city and were taught by professional historians, philosophers, and scientists. A few years later she married Pierre Curie, they discovered the powers of radioactivity, and got themselves on a French stamp and received a Nobel Prize for their work with radium. Pretty brave, eh?

If Marie Curie could overcome fear amidst so many obstacles, so can we. We can move from *fear* to *trust* by allowing ourselves the opportunity to take calculated, thoughtful risks. Not those foolish ones that usually involve a bottle of cheap wine and our ex-boyfriend's phone number, but the positive risks that can lead to greater personal success. By accomplishing our goals and overcoming fear, we learn that we are truly stronger than we ever knew.

Chellis lives in San Francisco and has spent over two years living and traveling by herself in various countries: China, Guam, Spain, South Korea, Japan, Saipan, Singapore, Thailand, Malaysia, Hong Kong, Macau, Germany, England, France, Tunisia, and Taiwan. (*Phew!*) I asked Chellis about her thoughts on fear and trust. "The issue of trust and fear is one that I think of often. Following your instincts is essential when it comes to traveling—and so is living without fear as your motivator. Although I took a fair amount of risks while on the road, I also took many conservative precautions. It all depended on my own feeling of safety in a particular place. In Spain, a laid-back, culturally open country, I had no qualms about being out alone until three a.m. But in a country like Tunisia, where the men were a bit aggressive, I was in my hotel room with the door locked when the sun set. Being adventurous is one thing; risking your life is another. But if I hadn't left fear behind, I wouldn't have been able to experience the world with such joy."

If you have any fear about flying solo, I suggest you to write them down and return to them after you finish this book. Perhaps you'll see your fear in a new light, or you'll learn that you are more powerful than your fears.

What are some of your fears about solo travel?

_____

_____

_____

_____

_____

_____

_____

List other words for *fear.*

_____

_____

_____

_____

_____

_____

_____

_____

To you, what is the opposite of *fear?* How can you find more of that?

_____

_____

_____

_____

_____

_____

_____

_____

> *"Nothing great in the world has ever been accomplished without passion."*
> – G.W.F. Hegel

The second piece of baggage we might want to leave behind when flying solo is laziness. Let's all make a commitment to go beyond our front doors and explore what the world has to offer. I love the following quote from Benjamin Disraeli, the nineteenth century English author and political activist: "Action may not always bring happiness; but there is no happiness without action." Unlike Marie Curie, we have the luxury of traveling freely—the world truly can be our "Flying University." We can't expect the Eiffel Tower or any of the many opportunities the world to show up at our doorstep.

Leaving fear and laziness behind is not just beneficial for travel— it's helpful for all aspects of life. Brian Tracy, one of my favorite life coaches, does an extraordinary job illustrating the source of laziness and procrastination in his excellent book *The Psychology of Achievement*. Tracy writes that a major reason for procrastinating is that tasks appear so large and formidable when we first approach them that we're afraid to start them. This can be true when we dream of traveling to a far-off location but don't know how to make our trip a reality. So often I hear, "I don't have a passport, I don't have a clue how to find a safe hotel, I really don't know where to start! Staying home is much easier."

One technique Tracy recommends to cut a big task down to size—what he calls the "salami slice" method of getting things done. With this method, you lay out the task in detail and then resolve to do just one slice of the job at a time. When planning a vacation, the first "slice" you need to "cut" is deciding what you want out of your trip. You've been working on that since chapter two! Take your time and explore your options. Start with a few locations that appeal to you, do some research, and see what resonates with you. No need to plunge in all at once. Psychologically, you'll find it easier to face a single, small piece of a large project than to arbitrarily dive in headfirst. Once you start researching and planning, you'll develop a sense of forward momentum and a feeling of accomplishment. You'll become energized and excited, and you'll feel motivated to keep going until your vacation is planned.

It takes time and effort to design the trip you want—and by being proactive and carefully researching your destination, you're able to wrestle away fears that can result from the unknown. You're no longer entering a situation that, in the past, would have caused you to be fearful. You're moving towards your future with knowledge, passion, and understanding.

Now that you have started this exciting process, what is the first step you need to take?
1. Decide to go!
2. Explore possible destinations.
3. Research each destination.
4. Figure out how you want to travel (tour, semi-solo, solo).
5. Pick a date.
6. Find an airline ticket.
7. Find a hotel or book the resort/tour/etc.
8. Let's keep going!

_____

_____

_____

_____

_____

_____

_____

"Pride sullies the noblest character."
– Claudianus Mamertus

According to Charles Panati's fascinating *Sacred Origins of Profound Things*, the Greek monastic theologian Evagrius of Pontus was the first person to devise a list of what he believed were the eight offenses and wicked human passions. They were, in order of increasing seriousness, gluttony, lust, greed, sadness, anger, sloth, vanity, and pride. (Been there, committed those!) Each of these offenses escalated in severity by an increased obsession with the self, pride being the most egregious. Pride, above all, robs us of our ability to rely on others and show gratitude. In Dana Facaros and Michael Paul's book *The Travelers' Guide to Hell*, they note that once you get on the pride wagon, you can kiss your chance of support goodbye, because pride says, "I know best, so just shut up."

Because I used pride as a self-defense mechanism, this was a lesson I had to learn the hard way. Any time I felt threatened or worried, I would pretend I was better, smarter, and more in control than anyone else. A darling older lady (in a to-die-for mink coat) in a New Orleans restaurant put it best when, after observing my abominable behavior with a boyfriend, told me, "You're tripping over your own pride darling, and that's not very graceful." Ouch! I knew she was right—and after my soon-to-be-ex stormed out during dessert, I was stuck with the dinner bill too. As Voltaire poignantly said, "We're rarely proud when we are alone." After my boyfriend left me at dinner, all my pride was definitely gone. So was $200 out of my back account for the meal I just ruined!

So pack those bags, remember to bring plenty of darling undies, comfy socks, and colorful scarves. And be sure to leave that other stuff we talked about in this chapter at home! Girl, you got a lot of traveling to do...so you'd better travel light.

Is there any other "sins" that you want to avoid when on your great adventure?

Remember: gluttony, lust, greed, sadness, anger, sloth, vanity, and pride.

Are there situations that cause these "sins" to appear? For me, it is when people cut me off or treat me with disrespect. I get angry. Now that I know that, I try to take a deep breath and think, "This person could be having a really bad day. Let it go."

What can you do if you feel that you are being triggered?

Teresa Rodriguez

Make a commitment to be a fabulous first class jetsetter:

_____
_____
_____
_____
_____
_____
_____
_____

I, _____, will strive to be a kind, peaceful world traveler by doing the following:

_____
_____
_____
_____
_____
_____
_____
_____

CHAPTER 5

Be Beautiful

*"Though we travel the world over to find the beautiful,
we must carry it with us or we find it not."*
– Ralph Waldo Emerson

"I have no idea where she came from, nor could I tell how old she was—she was truly timeless and beautiful. She was sitting at a window seat in a restaurant, sipping wine and eating her lunch in sheer delight—all by herself. She looked like she owned the place, lounging there in her beautiful outfit and perfectly coiffed hair. I wanted to be her and feel the confidence she exuded."

- Agatha, Dublin

Like my credit cards and good shoes, I carry a few important universal laws when I travel.

I have outlined here what like to call The Solo Manifesto.

Be confident, sister.

Walk in the room like you own the place! Stand tall and be present in your environment. For example, when you dine alone, don't just be a diner—be a reviewer.

Marya Charles Alexander, editor and publisher of SoloDining. com, writes, "Forget room service. Having a good time while dining out alone is easier than you think. Whether you're traveling for business or pleasure, mealtime should be fun time and an adventure."

Choose your restaurant and where you sit with care. Delight in picking up free cooking tips? Check out the growing array of restaurants offering chef's counters that cozy up to the kitchen. Besides getting a taste of how restaurants work, you'll find yourself kibitzing with culinary kings and queens, as well as with kindred counter-diners.

Connecting with other simpatico solo diners is always a pleasant possibility when you treat yourself to a meal out. Besides chef's counters, there are other ways to enhance the probability. Ask your hotel concierge about local restaurants that facilitate shared table seating for solo diners. This seating style ranges from intimate (a table for two) to grand (seating for thirty or more). As beloved by couples and groups as it is by solos, communal table dining is an incredible way to share a meal and often gives singles an opportunity to meet with locals. A terrific bonus!"

My friend Stephanie always talks about her favorite share tables at Duke's Canoe Club in Waikiki. These wide wooden tables of delight are the perfect place to sit your bikini-ed booty down amidst all those yummy off-base military men. She never has to pay for drinks and is always regaled with wild tales of exotic international posts. Not a bad way for a girl to spend an evening!

Dining out alone offers many opportunities, but one of the most satisfying is the chance for self-celebration. Eat what you want, when you want it! Make a meal of hors d'oeuvres or desserts. Just enjoy and allow others to minister to *you* for a change. Bon appetite!

Entertain yourself! Bring something to read, such as your beautifully disguised travel guides, local newspapers, and any free city guides you can find with nightlife and entertainment listings. Also, ask for a seat by the door for a good view of who's coming and going. My favorite seats in warm weather are outside near the entrance. I get to watch tourists, check out the local fashions, and absorb the authentic atmosphere. And don't forget your journal! These are the moments you'll want to record and remember.

> *"A loving person lives in a loving world. A hostile person lives in a hostile world.*
> *Everyone you meet is your mirror."*
> – Ken Keys

Be understanding, love.

First, seek to understand—because you never really know what's going on in others' lives. As much as you might want to slap that nasty salesperson, they might actually have a good reason for being so rude.

Sheila shares, "I was on a flight to Las Vegas when my perspective of life and people completely shifted. I was sitting next to a man who looked like he hadn't slept for a week, along with his annoying daughter who proceeded to kick the back of the seat in front of her, cry, and crawl around her dad's legs. The father just stared blankly into space. All I could think was, 'What a loser, this guy must be a crack-smoking gambler who brings his daughter to Vegas on the weekends he gets custody.' Luckily the flight was a short one from Los Angeles, because by the end of it I was about to slap both of them. I did a great job not saying a word. Thank God. Because the girl started repeating, 'I want to see mommy now, are we going to see mommy now?' Her dad answered, 'We're going to see grandma now.' And the girl went on, 'But I want to see mommy NOW.' Her dad gently held her shoulders, looked at her with all that was in him and said, 'Darling, mommy went to heaven a few days ago, remember? We're going to see grandma now.'"

> *"Our patience will achieve more than our force."*
> – Edmund Burke

Be patient, darling.

People's attitudes toward time are different throughout the world. Keep in mind that a New York minute is nowhere near Hawaiian time. Sometimes it's good to just sit back and chill (preferable with a glass of champagne!)
Marla sat comfortably in the wicker seat in front of the Barcelona café along the bustling Las Ramblas. She had been there for two hours, sipping and savoring a crimson glass of sangria. This was unlike the Marla who runs a manufacturing firm in Texas. Two and a half hours in her hectic real life was a very long time—things could change drastically if one of the conveyer belts stopped working, a packaging machine failed, or if she gave up any ground in numerous employee battles. Here in Spain, however, she was on vacation, and slowed her pace to match that of her surroundings.

"On my first trip to Europe, I thought I was going to go stir crazy. I couldn't understand why it took so long to get a coffee or small bite to eat. I went insane waiting for service. Now, I understand that this is part of the charm here. Now, not only do I respect it—I appreciate it! I have learned the art of patience, which I now utilize it in my daily life. I don't have to go into a frenzy when the line at the grocery store doesn't move; it's okay if it takes longer than I expect to get a meal. This was something I learned through travel. Not everyone is on Marla-time."

"God grant me the serenity to accept the things I cannot change,
the courage to change the things I can,
and the wisdom to know the difference."
– Reinhold Niebuhr

Be attractive, princess.

It's that fabulous "I'm looking good!" vibe that shows off your radiance and beauty: your attitude and energy, not your makeup and clothing. Be that spectacular lady everyone respects and swoons over.

While in Rome, be *La Dolce Vita* fabulous! Even if you're not the outgoing cheerleader everyone loves at the office, be her now! Be all those wonderful, charismatic, friendly attributes you admire in others. Make a list of all the people you adore and list the attributes you admire in them, and then take a piece of them with you when you travel. You too can have the style of Grace Kelly, the kindness of Mother Teresa, the beauty of Audrey Hepburn, and the sass of Dolly Parton!

List some of the people you admire and why:

_____

_____

_____

_____

_____

_____

_____

_____

"Wherever your journey takes you, there are new gods waiting there,
with divine patience—and laughter."
– Susan M. Watkins

Be positive, beautiful.

Smile. Be open to others and their cultures, and let them become part of you. Leave everyone you meet with a kind word.

In Dale Carnegie's classic *How to Win Friends and Influence People*, the second fundamental technique he writes about is the importance of smiling. "This simplest way to make a good first impression is to smile." This truth is very important when you travel. Even when you are in a foreign land where everyone speaks a different language than you, there is no doubt what a smile signifies. Carnegie writes, "Actions speak louder than words, and a smile says, 'I like you.' You make me happy, I am glad to see you." I'm not saying you need to be overly ebullient and enthusiastic, but you should show friendliness and confidence when engaging others. Be the person everyone wants to meet. Have a bounce in your step, a smile on your face, and glow with friendliness. By the time you leave town, everyone will be wondering, "What's her secret?"

Body language is an important component to your success—in life and as a traveler. When talking with others, make eye contact, smile, nod your head, and mirror their behavior. In other words, be a lady and respect your company. Dress yourself up in the natural excitement and wonder that comes from travel! You did it, you're here; it's amazing to be out in the world! Don't be afraid to let that out. Locals love it when a visitor is excited to be there, so engage the locals with their favorite topic: their home town! Even if you aren't outgoing at home, your travel self can be! After all, traveling isn't just about places—it's about people too. Including you!

And, because it is people who can ultimately enrich, deepen, and personalize your stay, it's a good idea to try not to inadvertently offend anyone. The meaning of hand gestures, for instance, varies widely from country to country. So do body language and clothing. Being a positive force in the destination of your choice involves doing a little research before you go. Language skills go a long way, too. Throwing out a "please" or "thank you" in a country's native tongue goes a long way in endearing people to you. If you make an effort with them, perhaps they will make an effort with you: like directing you away from the tourist path to a great café or small hidden church, mosque, or synagogue. While traveling, good etiquette falls somewhere between being curious and donning the manners you only use when going to visit your dear old great aunt Petunia in Charleston.

"Being solitary is being alone well: being alone luxuriously immersed in doings of your own choice, aware of the fullness of your own presence rather than the absence of others."
– Alice Koller

Happiness is not a destination that's beyond an ocean or a first-class ticket away. I've learned that happiness resides in me, especially when I'm wearing a fabulous pair of shoes and sporting my best smile. And it's through all these fantastic solo adventures that I've been able to explore who I am and what it means to be a part of a global community and a true travel Diva. I hope that wherever I go, I can learn something interesting from a stranger or even make a friend. You know those leave-a-penny-take-a-penny trays? Traveling is like that too—take an impression; make an impression. Mahatma Gandhi was right on target when he said, "You must be the change you wish to see in the world."

I was with my daughter in San Francisco when another mom was standing on the corner yelling for a quarter for her parking meter. The meter expired while she was loading her newborn baby in the car. The meter maid came up behind her car and started writing her a ticket and she was on the verge of tears. Dozens of people stopped and reached into their pocket and filled the meter for her. If that did not happen, she would have ended up with at $65 ticket. Yes, let's be the change.

List some actions that others did for you that made you feel better about yourself.

_____
_____
_____
_____
_____
_____
_____

List some things that you have done for others. How did that make you feel?

_____

_____

_____

_____

_____

_____

_____

_____

CHAPTER 6

Be Generous

"Love has nothing to do with what you are expecting to get—
only with what you are expecting to give—which is everything."
– Katherine Hepburn

"I was working as a waitress for a few months before I started my
Masters program in a college town far from home. I found it so darn
frustrating when I would work my hardest to serve a table and they would
leave little or no tip. On one particularly rough Sunday afternoon, I served
a quiet, older woman who ordered lunch and read her book in silence.
After she left, I cleaned her table and found a twenty-dollar tip with a
note that read, 'You remind me of me when I went back to school. Keep
up the hard work.' That tip changed my life. It was not only the money; it
was the fact that someone recognized the service I was doing. Since then,
everywhere I travel, I make sure to leave good tips."
- Sheila, New York

I admit it: I love first class, valet service, and pool boys. Room
service, spa treatments, and concierge assistance are all part of the

lexicon of travel that I adore. There's nothing so divine as pulling up to a five-star hotel and sending the bellboys into a flurry as they run to grab my luggage and get it to my room with the 500-count cotton sheets. I just love sitting poolside while the staff asks me if I want another piña colada. Of course I do!

But somewhere between the luggage and the colada, I realized that there was more to traveling than my own happiness. (Yeah, I know, hard to swallow!) It took me a few years of traveling to realize that those bellboys have families they support, and all those taxi drivers have people who love them too. It was in the midst of this epiphany that I realized I had a responsibility to all those souls who cared for me while I traveled, and that it was up to me to also share with them abundance and happiness. Yes, it is up to us to give others the same abundance we enjoy.

I challenge you to rethink your travel ideology and go beyond the boundaries of *receiving* and reflect on the art of *giving*. When we extend our kindness and generosity globally, we tap into a powerful force that transfers positive energy to others. We're not just giving a bigger-than-usual tip; we're offering a form of recognition for a job well done and an appreciation of good service. (The big tip does help though!) We become the conduits of good news and good thoughts. No longer are we tourists who are served but resented; we become soulful energy that brings gifts of love, thoughtfulness, and generosity. Our simple acts of giving create a light that shines on others and brings joy to all the lives we touch through our simple act of traveling. Imagine that you are a world ambassador for peace and generosity, and your job is to give generously—of your money, your time, your patience, your kindness, and your grace—and to not expect anything in return. Could you imagine the joy you would bring others?

*"You find true joy and happiness in life when you give
and give and go on giving and never count the cost."*
— Eileen Caddy

My friend Maria is one of the most giving women I know. And although she'll be the first to buy a round of drinks or pay for a cab, her generosity spans far beyond cash. She gives of her time with grace and willingness, and always with a smile. If I need something, I know that I can rely on Maria to help me out. She's quick with a "Is there anything I can help you with?" or an "I can do that for you." And it is those kind gestures that make my life easier, fun, and pleasant. Maria is my light in my world that sometimes gets dark, and I know that when I see her, she'll brighten my day. I look forward to seeing her any chance I can. I love being with her, and I know that I can count on her when I need a word of encouragement or piece of advice. It is the small things that really count, so no need to buy a dozen roses for the concierge, a kind word, a lovely tip, a thank you card. Those are all acts of generosity and kindness.

Start small at first. Try giving a bigger tip than usual or give someone a big "Thank you!" Don't expect to turn into Mother Teresa or the Dalai Lama after one quick trip. It takes time and practice to give so openly. Even before your trip, try with one act of giving a day, and strive towards a lifestyle where everywhere you go you give generously. Buy a round of drinks, offer to pay more than your share, or feel like a movie star when you say, "Keep the change!"

These are just a few ways that you can start being generous. At the end of your trip, leave all your change in the hotel room for the maid service, or give your change to one of the charities at the airport. A lot of airlines have UNICEF envelopes for you to purge your wallet of all those unwieldy foreign currencies you've collected. Clean your wallet and help a child. You will be amazed at all the opportunities the universe gives you to share your wealth. Remember too that wealth is relative; what seems like a small amount to you may mean the world to someone else.

If you're not in a position to give cash, give of yourself. Perhaps you're saying, "Sounds great, but how and when do I give?" I say, give when it feels right, give when it's uncomfortable, give when you have nothing left to give—and watch as your life is transformed by your willingness to connect with something greater. Take this journey as a chance to open up, and seek opportunities to give to others and help out. Perhaps you're at the airport and a mother with a few rambunctious children needs help with her carry-on: give her a hand. Perhaps an elderly man is having trouble getting out of his seat: give him a warm smile and your patience. Or perhaps you're sitting next to a child flying alone for the first time with one of those humongous plastic ticket holders around his or her neck. When my friend Stephanie found herself next to a child on his first solo flight, she put down the magazine she was looking forward to reading and introduced herself. Noticing that he was hanging onto his Game Boy® for dear life, she asked him about the game he was playing. An hour later, the boy was still enthusiastically coaching her on her gaming skills, totally unaware that the plane had touched down. Give your smiles away generously and show kindness in times of despair. Be the light you seek to find.

What does giving feel like to you right now?

_____

_____

_____

_____

_____

_____

What about sharing scares you?

_____
_____
_____
_____
_____
_____
_____
_____

What are you willing to give at first?

_____
_____
_____
_____
_____
_____
_____

If you were rich, what would you give? And to whom?

_____
_____
_____
_____
_____
_____
_____

> *"The most powerful thing you can do to change the world, is to change your own belief about the nature of life, people, reality, to something more positive…and begin to act accordingly."*
> – Shakti Gawain

You might ask yourself, "What am I going to get out of all this giving?" My favorite author, Dr. Wayne Dyer, explains the power of giving and its rewards in his *The Power of Intention*. "The more you give of yourself, no matter how little, the more you open the door for life to pour in. This not only compensates you for your gifts, it also increases the desire to give, and consequently the ability to receive as well. Make giving a way of life. "Trees bend low with ripened fruit; clouds hang down with gentle rain; noblemen bow graciously. This is the way of generous things." This powerful truth is one that we can take with us everywhere we go, along with the knowledge that the abundance we give will come back to us.

My aunts are the perfect examples for living in a state of giving and abundance. They're never short of a laugh and are always ready to prepare a delicious Mexican feast for anyone in need. Since I was a child, I have watched these women give. From cooking meals for others to driving sick friends to the doctor, these women are beyond generous. And through their generosity, they have touched lives, brought happiness to others—and even given me the confidence to write this book.

Are you usually generous with your money, time, or resources? In not, what fear is holding you back?

_____

_____

You'll find that through giving, you'll connect to a greater purpose, and learn how important you are to the universe. You are needed, you are loved, and you are respected. This will become clear when you start to experience the joy of giving without expecting. Your journey becomes a mission to find opportunities to assist others and not just the search for a wonderful solo vacation (which, now that you've read this book, is a given!) You'll soon see how your small impact can change the energy of the world to something positive and important. Your heart takes over and you'll revel in a sense of belonging and a sense of peace. You feel connected to other cultures, other attitudes, and other ideologies. You'll see that we are all part of one great global village—and that we all desire love, peace, and joy.

When you're in this place of generosity, others reach out to you with their gifts. From impromptu dinner invitations to warm hospitality, you'll find the world sharing its abundance with you. This was one of the first truths I learned when I started traveling alone. I went to London without making any hotel or hostel reservations, and when I got to town, it was a nightmare trying to find a place to stay each and every night. Instead of spending my days strolling through the museums or enjoying afternoon tea at Harrods, I searched for my next place to sleep that night, my backpack falling off my sore back.

I got off the tube at Piccadilly Circus, where a musician played the flute in one of the tunnels that lead to the outside world. His music was enchanting, and echoed through the dreary labyrinth of passageways, resting gently on my tired mind. Even though I was stressed out and short of money, I stopped to listen, smiled, and gave him a few quid. The second the coins hit his worn velvet hat I remembered that a year ago I helped an English friend of a friend who was stuck in San Francisco and needed a place to stay. I let him sleep on my couch for a few nights before his departure back to London. The very moment I dropped the coins in the hat, I remembered that he said that if I ever came to London I should look him up and he would let me stay with him. There was light at the end of the tunnel! I believe that the only reason I remembered this was because I took the time to stop, listen, and give. I looked up his name in the phone book and, just as he promised, he let me stay with him for a few nights—which was my saving grace! If I had not shown him kindness in his time of need, he would never have had the opportunity to show me kindness. This is the power of attraction. Like attracts like. I was so grateful to have a free couch to sleep on, and only blocks away from Harrods! It was then that I made the promise: any friend who needs a place to stay will have a place to stay with me. My door is always open.

> *"Like attracts like. Whatever the conscious mind thinks*
> *and believes, the subconscious identically creates."*
> – Brian Adams

So if you find yourself totally overwhelmed wandering through the streets of Calcutta flanked on every side with beggars and wondering what in the world you could possibly do to help, then Brava, Diva! The fact that you *want* to help—that you aren't even remotely satisfied with what you see—is huge. That's your generous spirit talking (or complaining)! When you get back home from Calcutta, Rio, Johannesburg, or South Central L.A., harness your discomfort into action!

There are millions of things to do, like committing to give regularly to a foreign charity, supporting the places you visit with kind thank-you letters, and by sharing your fabulous experience with others—by helping others to travel or sharing all the goodness of your trip with the world through writing or blogging. Don't keep a good thing to yourself! If you're up to big love service, consider volunteering for the Peace Corps, in an orphanage, or on a mission. There are a ton of great volunteer vacations out there. Just google "volunteer vacations' and you'll be overwhelmed by the opportunities to save turtles in Costa Rica or teach children in Sir Lanka!

From the simple act of genuinely saying "thank you" to becoming a volunteer in a third-world country, from volunteering internationally, to leaving a few extra pennies on the table, there are plenty of ways to give. You are needed in this world, and every bit helps: so go out there, and let your light shine!

"The most difficult thing—but an essential one—is to love Life, to love it even while one suffers, because Life is all. Life is God, and to love Life means to Love God."
– Tolstoy, *War and Peace*

How do you see yourself giving while on your journey? Money, time, patience, smiles?

_____

_____

_____

_____

_____

_____

Teresa Rodriguez

Does volunteering on vacation interest you? If so, what types of trips?

_____

_____

_____

_____

_____

_____

_____

Is there anything you can do locally to start your acts of giving?

_____

_____

_____

_____

_____

_____

_____

CHAPTER 7

Be Soulful

"Time has been transformed, and we have changed; it has advanced and set us in motion; it has unveiled its face, inspiring us with bewilderment and exhilaration."
– Kahlil Gibran

"I went away for ten days after my chemotherapy. What a gift it was to spend time alone. It was the first time I engaged in internal conversations and listened to my body. And WOW, my body had plenty to tell me! 'SLOW DOWN, LOVE ME, FEED ME.' This solo vacation was the catalyst for change in my life. I came back home transformed."
- Rebecca, Glasgow

When you return home after a solo vacation, I hope you'll discover that your home is cozier than when you left it, your friends and family missed you more than you expected, and that your job is still there. Not much has changed in your day-to-day life—except you.

My wish for you is that you no longer view your world with the same perspective as you did before. The smell of hot sand or the sight of a cute guys speeding on a Vespa will conjure fabulous new memories of the time you spent exploring the world alone. Perhaps you'll remember the generous waiter with a mischievous smile who served you that delicious glass of champagne gratis, or you'll recall that beautiful Italian woman who complimented you on your hair. And with these whispers of your trip, you'll be filled with the warmth of those timeless moments.

I'm not a gardener, but I find seeds to be the most interesting things around. They are these lifeless, dull bits that can turn into something fruitful and colorful. Sometimes I think our lives are like seeds, things that must first fall from their trees to find their way deep into the earth; once grounded, they must break to grow into beautiful plants that bloom with life and fruit. This is solo travel in a nutshell, every pun intended! You must first let go of everything that's safe; once you do, you will find yourself in a heady plunge straight into the great, wide world. This is you growing and changing. And in this growth, your seed bursts and your new life starts the minute you leave home. You now know what it's like to sleep under different stars and dream in distant lands. Congratulations!

"I am the woman who holds up the sky.
The rainbow runs through my eyes,
The sun makes a path to my womb.
My thoughts are in the shape of clouds.
But my words are yet to come."
– Poem of the Ute Indians

I trust that after your journey, you'll be filled with a new sense of confidence you didn't know was possible before your trip. And hopefully, because you overcame your fears, you see that life's obstacles are not the end of the world, just slight hiccups for which you will find solutions. And it would be great if with your newfound confidence you're more patient, because you know things will work out, one way or another. And if things didn't go exactly as you planned, I believe that you became skilled at being flexible and problem solving. This journey was just the beginning. And with any luck, you learned that you're stronger than you thought and that your life is bigger, grander, and more important than you expected it to be.

Maybe your luggage was heavy, but your heart was light. Perhaps you discovered more about yourself than you knew before you departed. You learned that you look beautiful strolling down a cobblestone path wearing a colorful silk scarf or that the sun on your face is all the blush you need. You learned how confident you can be under pressure, and how important a smile is. I bet you can now say "thank you" in three languages because you practiced thoughtfulness and shared your abundance with the world. What an adventure!

BODY

> *"It is good to have an end to journey toward,*
> *but it is the journey that matters in the end."*
> – Ursula K. LeGuin

Girl, did you need some time to rest, or were you running on all twelve chrome-polished cylinders? Let me guess, some days you enjoyed a quiet afternoon alone in the sun; other times you danced the night away in sheer happiness, your hair plastered to your face with the sweat of a balmy night? Wasn't it great not worrying about anyone's expectations but your own? Who really cared if you danced with that short Cuban guy all night long, or if you slept in until housekeeping called to ask if you wanted your sheets changed? I really hope that you liberated your body from its boring, daily routine. If you didn't want to work out, you didn't–right?

Sometimes coming back from a trip all refreshed is what you need. But, hey, if you need a vacation because of your vacation, then call in sick for a few days. Because we spend so much time pleasing others and listening to the needs of others, we forget to turn into the body channel and take a moment for the station identification. Hopefully you tuned in and listened. When I travel alone, I get so excited about all I want to do that I just can't sleep. I know this about myself, so I always plan a few days at home to recuperate from my jet-setting, disco-dancing ways.

Yes, you've enjoyed time away with the most important person in your world—you! Remember to always treat her well, take care of her needs, buy her dinner, and allow her to grow and explore. Fall in love with her again and again. Just because you're home doesn't mean you should stop treating her with kindness and respect.

How do you feel after your trip? Did your body talk to you and did you listen? Did it tell you something you didn't expect?

_____

_____

_____

_____

_____

_____

_____

_____

MIND

> *"To see a world in a grain of sand,*
> *And a heaven in a wild flower,*
> *Hold infinity in the palm of your hand,*
> *And eternity in an hour."*
> – William Blake

Occasionally, the one thing we want to leave at home is all those insane thoughts that drive our daily lives crazy. Thoughts like, "Did I turn off the iron, where did I leave my phone, or how come this Excel worksheet won't save?" Hopefully you got the opportunity to live in the *now* and to leave all of those mind-bending thoughts at home. Did you allow your intellect and imagination the chance to think through issues and situations that might not come up in your daily life, like, "Should I go to the Van Gogh museum today while it's still open, or should I check out a canal tour? Do I want to eat in a small café in the heart of the action, or do I want to stroll through the botanical gardens with a drawing pad and see what inspires me?" I bet it took a bit more mind power and creativity to sort through your fanciful options. "Should I talk to the cute guy with an English accent, or is that darling Italian more my type?" Decisions, decisions! I've discovered that trying to come to terms with multiple outcomes is a very powerful way to keep my mind active and healthy. And much more fun than crossword puzzles!

> *"Live out of your imagination, not your history."*
> – Stephen Covey

I'm optimistic that during your adventure, you began to trust your inner voice and imagination. Perhaps you listened to your thoughts and decided to do something spontaneous like order gelato and forget about the calories, or buy a bouquet of fabulous flowers for your hotel room. Did you begin to rely on your own intuition and sixth sense? Were you drawn to some people and not to others? You felt a connection with a lovely Spanish girl from Barcelona, but really didn't feel comfortable around the older lady from Rome? And in those overwhelming moments when you needed to make quick decisions, did you think of your options and work out solutions? Should you jump on the tube to Piccadilly or is Elephant Castle where you want to go? I think that sometime we forget how much we know and what we are truly capable of doing. I find that solo travel gives me a chance to discover how immeasurable my knowledge truly is, and how intensely I can trust myself.

What were some of the "mind moments" you experienced? Did your mind say things to you that surprised you? Did you let your imagination soar, and if so, where did it take you?

_____

_____

_____

_____

_____

_____

_____

_____

SOUL

> *"Love that moment, and the energy of that*
> *moment will spread beyond all boundaries."*
> – Corita Kent

Some of my favorite moments are when I let the world speak to me. Did she speak to you? Did you hear the soulful songs that ride on the billows of creation and celebration? Like the soft sound of rain beating on stone streets at dawn, or your name being whispered from the sweet lips of a gorgeous Brazilian man? This trip was about more than just finding the best hotel or dining on delicious food: it was about finding your strength and reconnecting with your exhilarating spirit. Chances are that you revealed to the world how strong you truly are, and you learned how much the world supports your desires. You're more than your magnificent body; you're greater than your imprecise height, or vague age. You are ever expansive and glorious, and forever connected to the world.

My wish is that you'll always remember the local children who helped you scramble through the temples of Angkor Wat and who knew more about this sacred space than your guide. And I trust you'll remember that the cherry blossoms in Kyoto were the softest pink you ever saw, and that roast chicken after an entire day of white water rafting never tasted so delicious. These moments of remembrance keep us connected to something bigger than our credit card bills and split ends. When I'm on the edge, or feeling down, I try to find time and take a moment to reconnect with those fantastic moments I've experienced on my travels. When I do, I gain perspective quickly on my life, and I always end my brief meditation with a big grin and sometimes a giggle. How can you not be happy when thinking about that perfect walk through the jungle in Thailand with only the sounds of butterfly wings and your breath?

While traveling alone, did unexpected miracles occur and lovely serendipitous moments spring up like green fairies? Did the perfect people enter your life as if on cue? For me, the perfect seat in a sidewalk café will open up just as I saunter by, or I'll run into someone that needs to be in my life at that moment. One time, in Amsterdam, a guy riding on a bicycle in front of me lost his bag and I stopped to help him. He turned out to be a personal shopper who spent the day showing me fascinating parts of Amsterdam that tourists never get to experience. His name is Harry and it's been over six years since then, but we still stay in touch. Friendships like this make the world a smaller, safer place filled with hope and possibilities.

What soulful moments will you always remember from this trip?

_____

_____

_____

_____

_____

_____

_____

_____

What miracles did you experience?

_____

_____

_____

_____

_____

_____

_____

_____

YOUR STORY

"The artist, a traveler on this earth,
leaves behind imperishable traces of his being."
— François Delsarte

Remember in high school we learned that our identities, rituals, and history were passed down from generation to generation via storytelling and pictures. Important and powerful moments were captured on walls of caves and transmitted through myths. And just like those caves filled with remarkable drawings of buffalos, your journey is a mighty expression of your success in this world—share it and celebrate it! Take time to capture it through creative outlets like journaling, blogging, photography, drawing, and poetry. Get a big album worthy of your memories and fill it to the brim with your swashbuckling tales. Or start a blog that you can share with the world. Who knows, you just might inspire someone else who needs a bit of a nudge.

When on my trips, I try to pick up a journal from that destination and spend time each day capturing my thoughts on its pages. Collecting your memories and showcasing them in a beautiful book is one of the best ways to chronicle your growth and personal experiences from your glorious adventure, not to mention a great way to keep track of those great restaurants and hotels you want to recommend to your friends. Honor your escapades and share your life-altering saga in a prized book you'll keep in a place of prominence in your home for all to read! Let your story say, "I've done it! I conquered my fears. I went beyond the bounds of mediocrity and set foot on new territory! I've experienced joys and wonder-filled moments that no one can take from me!" Don't be afraid to share your travel achievements with others. Let everyone know that solo travel can be overwhelming and challenging, but it's also incredibly rewarding and self-affirming.

The solo-travel torch is now in your hands, my friend—it's up to you to pass it on. Pass it with passion and resolve. Pass it with adoration and thoughtfulness. Pass it with a sense of responsibility to all the souls occupying this crazy planet. Through your personal storytelling, others will understand how profound your decision to go it alone was. In the act of solo travel you have become Brave, Bold, and Beautiful. Sometimes we take for granted all of our achievements, but your trip was one that will inspire others to explore the world too. Let others know you sojourned past stereotypes and stigmas. Sing to them about how you sailed past fear and pride, and how you arrived on the shores of beauty and adventure equipped with your sexy-fine little black dress and your international calling card. You don't need to tell them about that really cute guy you kissed...unless you want to.

Share a powerful decision you made on this trip.

_____
_____
_____
_____
_____
_____
_____
_____

What moment did you feel most alive?

_____
_____
_____
_____

_____

_____

_____

_____

How are you going to use this new experience to make positive changes in your life?

_____

_____

_____

_____

_____

_____

_____

What aspects of your life grew the most on this journey?

_____

_____

_____

_____

_____

_____

_____

Teresa Rodriguez

If you had to encourage someone who was afraid to conquer the world alone, what advice would you give her?

———————————————————————
———————————————————————
———————————————————————
———————————————————————
———————————————————————
———————————————————————
———————————————————————
———————————————————————

Congratulations! You've successfully conquered the world alone. So where are you off to next?

The End
Or just the beginning?

CPSIA information can be obtained at www.ICGtesting.com
Printed in the USA
LVOW08*0723130913

352066LV00001B/2/P